INTERNATIONAL GARDEN
PHOTOGRAPHER
OF THE YEAR

**WINNING IMAGES OF PLANTS, GARDENS,
WILDLIFE, PEOPLE AND LANDSCAPES**

INTERNATIONAL
GARDEN
PHOTOGRAPHER
OF THE YEAR

Awarded to

Helen Ashton

Finalist

Trees

In the International Garden
Photographer of the Year **competition**

2010

INTERNATIONAL GARDEN
PHOTOGRAPHER
OF THE YEAR

CONTENTS

A DAVID & CHARLES BOOK
Copyright © David & Charles Ltd, 2010

David & Charles is an F+W Media, Inc. Company
4700 East Galbraith Road Cincinnati, OH 45236

First published in the UK in 2010

Images © see page 160

A catalogue record for this book is available from
the British Library.

ISBN 13: 978-0-7153-3822-3 Hardback
ISBN 10: 0-7153-3822-6 Hardback

ISBN-13: 978-0-7153-3823-0 Paperback
ISBN-10: 0-7153-3823-4 Paperback

Printed in the UK by ButlerTanner & Dennis Ltd
For David & Charles Ltd
Brunel House, Newton Abbot, Devon, TQ12 4PU

Publisher: Stephen Bateman
Commissioning Editor: Neil Baber
Editorial Manager: Emily Pitcher
Editor: Verity Muir
Senior Art Editor: Nick Otway @ Alphaforme
Image retouching: Mike Moody
Design Manager: Sarah Clark
Proofreader: Hugh Brazier
Production: Bev Richardson

www.davidandcharles.co.uk

FOREWORD

Photograph by Rhian J Smith

I am delighted to be contributing the foreword to this book, *International Garden Photographer of the Year*, now in its third successful year.

The Royal Botanic Gardens, Kew is pleased to be hosting the accompanying exhibition again, displaying the work of the competition winners and finalists. The feedback from our visitors to the Gardens is that this is now a popular feature of our summer programme.

The wonderfully diverse range of quality images that make up this book does much to bring to the attention of the general public not only the aesthetic beauty but also the importance of plants in our environment.

This is especially relevant in 2010, since Kew, along with many other organisations, is celebrating the role of plants as part of the International Year of Biodiversity, a United Nations initiative aiming to promote the understanding of all aspects of diversity of life on earth.

The competition categories – covering plant portraits, wildlife and people in gardens, edible plants, and trees – vividly portray how plants and animals remain central to our well-being, in both practical and spiritual terms. This is also illustrated by images from MuckIn4Life; the campaign run by Defra aiming to increase the number and diversity of people involved in conservation volunteering.

We recognise that this competition actively encourages people of all ages to get out and engage with their environment, in different and inspiring ways – photography is a fantastic 'entry point' to wider issues of conservation and biodiversity.

Professor Stephen Hopper FLS, Director of the Royal Botanic Gardens, Kew

ABOUT THE COMPETITION

JUDGING

The judging of International Garden Photographer of the Year took place over a period of two months from December 2009 to February 2010. Every photograph was scrutinised and assigned a ranking by individual judges. These were then tallied and carried forward to a series of group judging sessions held at the studios of Andrew Lawson photography. High-resolution image files were then requested from short-listed entrants and another set of judging discussions and decisions took place. We thank all the judges for their dedication and thoroughness in assessing a very wide range of entries from all over the world.

JUDGES

Andrew Lawson
Garden photographer

Clive Nichols
Garden photographer

Heather Angel
Wildlife photographer

Tony Kirkham
Head of Arboretum and Horticultural Services at The Royal Botanic Gardens, Kew

Laura Giuffrida
Exhibition and Galleries Leader, Royal Botanic Gardens, Kew

Ray Spence
Lecturer in photography at Birmingham Institute of Art and Design

Victoria Skeet
Picture Editor, National Trust

Damien Demolder
Editor, *Amateur Photographer*

Tamsin Westhorpe
Editor, *The English Garden* magazine

THANKS

International Garden Photographer of the Year is organised by Philip Smith assisted by Mary Denton. They would like to thank the following for their help and support in creating this annual exhibition:

The Royal Botanic Gardens, Kew: David Yard, the press, marketing, estates and Festival teams

The National Trust at Lacock Abbey: Karen Bolger and Susan Carter

Little Green Monkey: Hagar Lee and Ben Waterson

The Royal Photographic Society: Liz Williams

Photobox: Linda Buttle

The Colour Studios team

Julie Kelly, Andrew Lawson, Judy Dod, Clive Nichols, Briony Lawson, Kerry Banner, Nick Otway, Neil Baber, Michael Moody, Hannah Whitworth, Clive Boursnell

Above all, the International Garden Photographer of the Year team thanks all the photographers who have entered the competition. Whether selected or not, their photographs have been a joy to see and a privilege to to share.

SPONSORS AND SUPPORTERS

The Royal Photographic Society was founded in 1853 to promote 'the Art and Science of Photography', a mission that continues to this day in the United Kingdom and through its considerable overseas membership.

Patron: Her Majesty The Queen.   Incorporated by Royal Charter

WORKSHOPS

International Garden Photographer of the Year runs workshops in association with the Royal Photographic Society. These are currently held at Lacock Abbey, Wiltshire, and Royal Botanic Gardens, Kew. The sessions are open to anyone who wants to improve their garden photography at whatever level of experience. We are indebted to leading garden photographer Clive Boursnell for his help in setting up and running these workshops.

Below: *International Garden Photographer of the Year at Wakehurst Place, Autumn 2009*

EXHIBITION

The International Garden Photographer of the Year exhibition opens each year in May at the Royal Botanic Gardens, Kew. The exhibition is displayed in a unique outdoor gallery enjoyed by many thousands of visitors. The exhibition then tours to Wakehurst Place, Sussex, and to Lacock Abbey, Wiltshire.

There are also satellite exhibitions at selected venues. In 2010 this includes Westonbirt Arboretum, Gloucestershire, The Alnwick Garden, Northumberland, and the Garden Museum, London.

www.igpoty.com

INTERNATIONAL GARDEN PHOTOGRAPHER OF THE YEAR

Gardens are where nature and humanity meet in harmony. The outcomes of that meeting can be glorious not only for the gardener but for every person who sees that garden. This competition and exhibition is a place where that glory is celebrated. Furthermore, it invites anyone with a camera to participate in that celebration. Our hope is that everyone who enters the competition – whether they win a prize or not – will feel that their own appreciation of gardens and plants has been heightened as a result of making their picture choices for the competition, inspiring them to try a new technique, or perhaps looking at plants in a different way.

Photographers were invited to enter single images or portfolios of six images in any of the following categories:

GARDEN VIEWS

Visiting a garden is a great day out for many of us. We can stand and admire the work of gardeners who have dedicated themselves to creating a personal paradise for the enjoyment of themselves and others.

Images could be submitted from gardens in any part of the world, from Tokyo and Cape Town to Glasgow and Melbourne. Photographers were invited to submit images that showed what is special about a particular garden, whether it is large or small, a chic design statement or a plantsman's paradise.

PLANT PORTRAITS

Achieving great images of plants and flowers requires skill, passion and commitment. This category celebrates the ephemeral beauty of the plant from seed to compost. Plant portraiture is all about capturing the very essence, or character, of a plant. This could be a rambling rose or a humble bluebell, an exotic tree peony or the delicate flowerhead of a grass. A single bloom in isolation can be admired for its uniqueness.

PEOPLE IN THE GARDEN

Gardens are for enjoyment – even if that enjoyment sometimes means hard work! Kids love to run around, while many of us will enjoy the round of the seasons – sowing, planting, clipping and harvesting. And then of course there's always that day when the garden is just for family and friends – good conversation or just plain relaxation. The judges looked for those pictures that really illustrate a passion for a personal retreat, a playground, or a workplace!

WILDLIFE IN THE GARDEN

In a world where natural habitats are being depleted, gardens are a haven for wildlife. The wild creatures that use our gardens can become familiar companions, or rare and special visitors. These may be creatures that only you are privileged to see – a nocturnal hedgehog, for example, or tiny insects that are easily overlooked, except by the keen photographer!

This category is all about the creatures that enjoy the garden, from beetles and butterflies to birds and badgers. These images display that moment where 'wildlife in the garden' becomes an inspiration.

THE EDIBLE GARDEN

Growing your own vegetables and fruit is more popular then ever. Whether it is carrots and cauliflowers or exotic fruits and herbs, we can all grow something to eat. The formal kitchen gardens of a bygone age provide many great photographic opportunities, as well as knot gardens full of herbs, old apple orchards, close-ups of seeds and fruit ripening in the sun – and don't forget the humble pot of tomatoes on the windowsill!

TREES

This category celebrates the tree in all its diverse forms. From the gnarled old oak to the mighty redwood, photographers were invited to show us how important trees are in our lives and in the health of our planet.

Winning images reveal the treasures of our great world forests as well as the beauty of a solitary tree. How do people and trees live side by side in one world? How does a tree create a sense of well-being? Most of all, these photographs celebrate the simple beauty of our planet's trees.

Below: *International Garden Photographer of the Year at Royal Botanic Gardens, Kew, 2009*

AWARDS

The title of **International Garden Photographer of the Year** was awarded to the best single image.

The **Best Portfolio** award was given to the best themed portfolio. Runner-up prizes were awarded to the portfolios judged second and third. A first, second and third award were given for each category. In addition, a number of photographs in each category were judged to be 'Finalist'. These and the winning photographs form the International Garden Photographer of the Year exhibition at the Royal Botanic Gardens, Kew, and other venues.

A number of photographs were also selected as 'Highly Commended' in each category. These appear on our website and are also published in this book.

Above: *International Garden Photographer of the Year at Royal Botanic Gardens, Kew, 2009.*

SPECIAL AWARDS

• Young Garden Photographer of the Year. Under 16s were invited to enter single images in any of the above categories.
• Spirit of the American Garden.

We hope that those who enter will learn and be inspired by the photographs that they see in this book and at the exhibition. We, as organisers, are ourselves inspired by the people we meet and speak to both at the exhibition and in the course of the competition year. The scenes depicted on these pages offer a pause for thought, a quietening of the breath, an opening of the eyes. Gardens are a haven not only for plants, not only for wildlife, but for us.

INTERNATIONAL GARDEN
PHOTOGRAPHER
OF THE YEAR

MARIANNE MAJERUS

◄ **MARIANNE MAJERUS**   FIRST

Layered Landscape: A Moment Captured
Private garden, Luxembourg.

Sunlight streams through the trees to *Actaea simplex* (Atropurpurea group), *Sedum spectabile* and grasses, and the layering of the mist over the fields in the distance provides a stage on which the plants perform their morning dance. The scene was utterly irresistible as the early morning light broke through the tree canopy and tickled the *Actaea*.

📷 Fuji Velvia 50, Leica R9

▲ **CLAIRE TAKACS**   Second

The Snake
James van Sweden's garden in Maryland, USA.

James was interested in the reflections of the black-eyed Susan (*Rudbeckia hirta*) flowers in the swimming pool. These flowers are native wildflowers to North America.

📷 Canon 1 Ds, 17–40mm, f/5.7

▲ **JEFF FRIESEN**

The Hidden Bridge

Portland Japanese Garden, Portland, Oregon, USA.

In Japanese tradition it is thought that crossing a zig-zag (or *yatsuhashi*) bridge helps one to avoid evil spirits, which flow in straight lines. I love Japanese Gardens and would happily photograph nothing else. I am inspired by the miniature, self-contained world formed by a Japanese garden. My approach was to frame the bridge so that it led the viewer through the photograph like a virtual garden stroll.

📷 **Canon EOS 5D, 24–105mm, f/14**

RACHEL WARNE   FIRST

The Present Past – A Forgotten Place

Pentille Castle kitchen garden, Pentille Castle, England.

Photographs of different areas within the old glasshouse in the walled kitchen gardens of Pentille Castle. I wanted to create a series of ethereal images for an intriguing point of view. I wanted them to look almost 100 years old, as if they were original pictures taken when the gardens were in their thriving state. Even though the garden has been forgotten, I think the way that nature and time have taken over makes for a very interesting photograph. It was like discovering a lost city.

📷 **Canon 5D Mark II, 24–105mm, wide**

◄ **TIM SMITH**

Winter at Elvaston Castle

Elvaston Castle, Derbyshire, England.

I've photographed the gardens at Elvaston several times and I am always drawn to the contrast between the geometric shape of the box hedging and the irregular, more 'organic' forms of the yew. On that day the snow topping seemed to further emphasise this distinction while the falling snow stippled and lightened the dark masses of the planting.

📷 **Canon 1 Ds Mark III, Canon 24–70mm f/2.8 at 70mm, f/7.1, 1/400sec**

I kept the shutter speed fairly high to capture the falling snow with just a little movement blur, and also to combat the fact that I was shaking like a leaf in the freezing cold!

▲ JOHN HINDE

Roald Dahl's Garden, Great Missenden

Gypsy House, Great Missenden, Buckinghamshire, England.

The garden has evolved since Roald Dahl's death in 1990, but one feature that remains is his writing hut, which has been preserved since he died. The obvious 'feature' in his garden is the gypsy caravan which he had restored (hence 'Gypsy House'), but it's been shot so many times. Instead I liked the pattern created by the bottles and thought that the combination of the two would make a good image.

📷 **Canon 350D, 18–55mm**

Images combined in image-processing software.

▲ **JONATHAN BERMAN**

The Dovecote

Eastcote House gardens, England.

The dovecote and the walled garden used to belong to Eastcote House, but it has long since been demolished and they are now public gardens. I frequently visit these attractive gardens on family walks, and I always try to have my camera with me as the best light doesn't usually last long. On this particular day the small walled garden looked at its best in the spring light.

📷 Canon G10 with infrared conversion, standard lens at 13.6mm, f/6.3

► CAROLE DRAKE

Old Rectory, Pulham, Early Autumn Morning

Old Rectory, Pulham, Dorset, England.

A perfect late October morning at the Old Rectory, with layers of mist rising off the Dorset countryside and the sky full of painterly cloud and colour. The formal elements of the garden – a box parterre containing standard laurels and *Santolina*, and yew pyramids – frame the rural view beyond.

📷 Nikon D200, Nikon 24–85mm at 24mm

JEFF FRIESEN

Far From Home

Tea-tinted photographs of Japanese gardens in North America

Portland, Oregon, USA; Vancouver, British Columbia, Canada; Victoria, British Columbia, Canada.

This portfolio features tea-tinted images of Japanese gardens that have been created on North America's west coast, across the Pacific Ocean from their traditional home in Japan. The photographs were made in springtime because I love the sense of energy in the air when plants awaken from winter dormancy.

📷 Canon EOS 5D, 24–105mm, between f/4 and f/14

▲ **DANNY BEATH**   Highly commended

Jardín Botánico Wilson

The Monocot Garden, Jardín Botánico Wilson, Costa Rica.

This photograph shows the rare specialist collection of monocots and bromeliads half-hidden in the morning mists and dripping with the abundant moisture of its cloud-forest habitat. I was inspired by images of the cloud forest around the gardens and wanted to create an almost Tolkien-like feel to my final shot, with moody silhouettes in the mist. I waited for a good fog to descend on the gardens before choosing my vantage point and using a tripod and two shots to create a distortion-free panorama of the misty gardens.

📷 Fuji Velvia 50, Nikon FE2, Nikkor 55mm, f/5.6

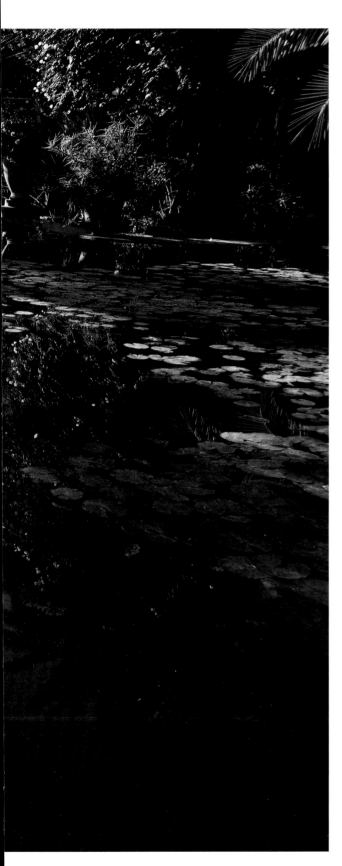

◄ **STEPHEN STUDD**

Majorelle Gardens, Marrakech, Morocco

Jardin Majorelle, Marrakech, Morocco.

Arriving at dawn, I wanted to capture the depth of the gardens, which work on many levels: the view across the pond towards various plantings, the sunlight filtering through, highlighting the water lilies and adding depth, palms reflected in the water and the cobalt blue surrounding the pool. With the wide-angle lens I wanted to depict the garden from its tallest point – the palms – to the plants around the pool, down to the water lilies.

📷 **Canon EOS 1Ds Mark II, Canon 24–70mm**

No tripods were allowed in the garden.

CLAIRE TAKACS   HIGHLY COMMENDED

Lotusland, Ganna Walska's fantasy gardens in mist

Lotusland, Santa Barbara, California, USA

Lotusland was the creation of Madame Ganna Walska, who purchased the 37-acre Santa Barbara estate in California in 1941. Her natural artistic talents and theatrical background were used to create a botanical garden of rare plants, and an extraordinary and beautiful fantasy world. Her vision was to develop Lotusland into the most outstanding centre of horticultural significance and educational use. Photographing one misty morning was, I believe, the ideal way to capture this garden's unique, surreal and otherworldly character.

   I made a visit to the gardens the day before I photographed to get an idea of what was there and to get a feel for the scale of the garden. I returned the next morning to photograph at first light, hoping for atmospheric conditions. I also arranged to be there on the day the gardens were closed to visitors, so I could experience the garden when it was quiet, and be free to photograph without people.

📷 Canon 1 D3, 17–40mm and 70–200mm

– Golden barrel cactus (*Echinocactus grusonii*) and large weeping *Euphorbia ingens* at the entrance to the late Madame Ganna Walska's residence.

– Succulents hanging from a tree in the main lawn, with misty background and trees beyond.

– Cactus gardens in mist.

– The original estate swimming pool was turned into a water garden with lotus and water lilies. The original bath house remains behind the pool, used today as a gardening shed.

– The path through Aloe Garden at Lotusland, containing over 120 different types of *Aloe*.

– The garden was designed with vision to be viewed at night with a full moon reflecting off the abalone shells.

◄ **MARIANNE MAJERUS**

Poppies at Dawn

Private garden, Norfolk, England.

On my way to the kitchen garden the early morning sun penetrated the fog which had enveloped the Norfolk marshes, and the sun's rays picked out the poppy flowers in a tranquil and secluded enclave of the garden. The morning mist rose, with a view toward the kitchen garden, and a clump of *Papaver rhoeas*. I positioned myself in order to benefit from the soft-filtered light breaking through the tree canopy.

📷 **Canon EOS 5D Mark II**

► **MARIANNE MAJERUS**   <small>FINALIST</small>

Stipa gigantea* Amongst *Betula utilis* var. *jacquemontii
The Manor House, Stevington, England.

The last light of the setting sun catches the grasses amongst the birch trees and the *Stipa gigantea* growing around the base of *Betula utilis* var. *jacquemontii*. I was inspired by the light effects – delicately backlit seed heads appearing to fall as golden rain among the solid and vertical birch trunks. Setting the effect against a dark background allowed the colours to appear more vivid.

📷 **Canon EOS 5D Mark II**

▲ DAVE DILGER

Swan Lake

Akashi Botanical Gardens, Japan.

Akashi is an industrial city in Hyogo Prefecture, southwest Japan. Sandwiched between Akashi train station and the 400-year-old Akashi Castle is a beautiful lake which is home to a number of swans. An avenue of fountains front the traditional botanical gardens and the main road, and it was sheer magic when the swans passed through the mist.

📷 Nikon D70, AF–S Nikkor 18–70mm, f/9

▲ LINDA WRIDE

Potting Shed

Tyntesfield, Wraxall, Somerset, England. By kind permission of the National Trust

A collection of garden sieves in different sizes adorn the wall above the potting bench in the seed store, where traditional terracotta and modern plastic flower pots are stacked ready for use, along with a container of plant supports and a mechanical dibber/press. Initially attracted by the striking arrangement of sieves on the wall and the patterns created by the different grades of mesh, I was drawn in by the diffuse light from the window illuminating a scene which has changed little since Victorian times, and wanted to capture that timeless atmosphere.

📷 Nikon D300, 16–85mm f/3.5–5.6, f/7.1

◄ **GERALD MAJUMDAR**   FINALIST

Sunrise at High View

The garden of Mike and Carole Dunnett at High View
in Worcestershire, England.

I was inspired by the sun shining through the trees and the composition with the pond, the
purple flowers and the small post-and-rail fence.

📷 Canon EOS 5D Mark II, Canon 24–70mm f/2.8, f/11

ANDREA JONES THIRD

Pools in American Gardens

Images 2,3,4,5,6 commissioned for the book *Great Gardens of America* by Tim Richardson, (Frances Lincoln, 2009)

📷 **Fuji Velvia RVP 135 and Fuji Velvia RVP 100, Leica RE, Fuji GX617 and Kodak DCS Pro SLR/n**

1– Baja Garden, Phoenix, Arizona. Design by Steve Martino.

2– Swimming pool with ornamental grass planting looking to Napa Valley, California. Gennets Garden, Napa, California. Design by Topher Delaney/SEAM Studios.

3– The Lovers' Lane Pool, Dumbarton Oaks, Washington DC.

4– The house and garden sit in the Sonoma Hills with a view over Sonoma. The swimming pool is set in paving and decking, framed by live oaks, (*Quercus virginiana*). The first kidney-shaped swimming pool.

5– Filoli Gardens, California.

6– The Aloe Garden at Lotusland, California with kidney-shaped swimming pool and fountain of giant clam shells.

3

4

5

6

◄ JOSE SHACKLETON FINALIST
Pinhole Summer Garden
Levens Hall, Kendal, Cumbria, England.

A wild jumble of daisies (*Bellis perennis*), forget-me-nots (*Myosotis scorpioides*), the odd dandelion (*Taraxacum officinale*), wild garlic flowers (*Allium ursinum*) and fresh green grass, set amidst a beech (*Fagus sylvatica*) hedge, an interwoven lattice of willow (*Salix*), and deciduous trees in the background. I wanted to capture the beauty of a garden that is so often overlooked, unnoticed, unseen in all its detail. This takes me back to my childhood and the way I remember the garden at home. I adopted a traditional approach and used film rather than a digital camera, and I nestled my pinhole camera in the grass to achieve the angle of view and perspective and took a few exposures on 120 roll film.

📷 **Zero 2000 pinhole camera, no lens, Fuji Pro 160 C, Pinhole size: 0.18mm, 1/138**
The 130-degree angle of view and depth of focus that pinhole affords greatly contributed to this image.

▲ CLAIRE TAKACS HIGHLY COMMENDED
Water Gardens at Lotusland
Loutusland, Santa Barbara, California, USA.

A beautiful misty morning at Lotusland. Garden designer and journalist Kate Frey highly recommended that I visit these gardens and photograph them. On the day I was completely inspired by the otherworldly, surreal atmosphere, enhanced by the mist. I visited the gardens at sunrise hoping for some early-morning atmospheric light, and I was absolutely delighted to find the morning mist, which went away later in the day. The original estate swimming pool now contains lotus and water lilies.

📷 **Canon 1 Ds, 17–40mm, f/8**

◄ **MARIANNE MAJERUS**

Morning Light on an Enchanting Tapestry of Flowers
Sleightholmedale Lodge, Yorkshire, England.

Early morning light filtering through tree canopy underplanted with *Meconopsis grandis* (Himalayan poppy), *Aquilegia vulgaris* and alliums. In the early morning light the scene was reminiscent of a delicate pastel embroidery of aquilegia, punctuated by Himalayan poppies, far from their homeland yet seeming completely at home in the Yorkshire countryside, skilfully naturalised by owner Rosanna.

📷 **Canon EOS 5D Mark II**

AWARD SPONSORED BY photob✿x.

► **MANDY DISHER**   FIRST

The beacon

Home studio.

My love of nature, especially flowers, has inspired me to strive to capture and share my view of its beauty. *Cosmos bipinnatus* 'Sonata Series' is such an elegant and beautiful flower, so I wanted to try to capture its wonderful ethereal qualities – its pure white flowing petals reaching up from the slender stem reminded me of a bright light in the dark.

These half-hardy annual plants are very easy to grow from seed. Ideal for the garden border, they can be arranged in groups for height and colour among other tall plants. They are also ideal for cutting, lasting well in water, and are appreciated for their long stems. They are undemanding plants and will flourish in warm sun and poor soils. The 'Sonata Series' produces compact plants with large red, pink and white flowers. The word *Cosmos* is derived from the Greek, meaning 'a balanced universe'.

📷 **Canon EOS 450D, Tamron 90mm Di Macro, f/11**

◄ **BRIAN HASLAM** Second

Magnolia campbellii 'Alba'

Cornwall, England.

The tree was stunning – full of perfect flowers conveniently situated at eye level. I held the front petal down with one hand to show the central pistil and stamens.

📷 Canon EOS 5D, Canon EF 24–105mm, f/9

▲ **SERGEY KAREPANOV** Third

Tulipa – Universe of Flowers

The Netherlands.

I grow tulips at home, but had never seen such an enormous amount of flowers as I found when I visited a Dutch polder full of tulips last spring. The sky is the only possible backdrop for a scene of such magnificence.

📷 Canon EOS 1 Ds Mark III, Canon EF 15 mm f/2.8

DAVID LOW FINALIST

Decaying Leaves on Water

Various nature parks in Singapore.

Leaf portraiture has always been my favourite, and whenever I'm walking in the park it's the first subject that I look out for. This portfolio captures the essence of their transformation of colours and textures as the leaves go through their awesome decay.

People tend to miss little things around us, but I like to observe the details. I find that decaying leaves are a subject that has been largely neglected by photographers – perhaps it is the state of deterioration that puts people off. Personally, I tend to find that even in its withering stage a leaf has beautiful colours.

📷 **Panasonic FZ–50, 35–420 kit lens**

3

4

5

6

1– Frozen Cookie
2– Never Alone
3– RGB
4– Computer Game (chomp chomp)
5– Loving Couple
6– Gliding Along

▲ KRISTIN LINNEA BACKE　　　　　　　　　HIGHLY COMMENDED

Queen Anne's Pocket Melon on the Prowl

Oslo, Norway.

I love colour, light and a feeling of transparency, as shown in this Queen Anne's pocket melon (*Cucumis melo var. dudaim*). Sometimes the camera feels a bit like a microscope. Nature's shapes are incomparable, both macroscopic and microscopic.

📷 Ricoh GX200

▶ CAROL SHARP　　　　　　　　　　　　　　FINALIST

Magical Umbellifer

Umbria, Italy.

This beautiful wild umbellifer was growing in profusion on a rough bit of land in Italy. I was entranced by the delicate, graceful and demure stance of the plant, beautifully demonstrating the network of tiny umbels.

📷 Nikon 200, Nikkor 70–300, f/5

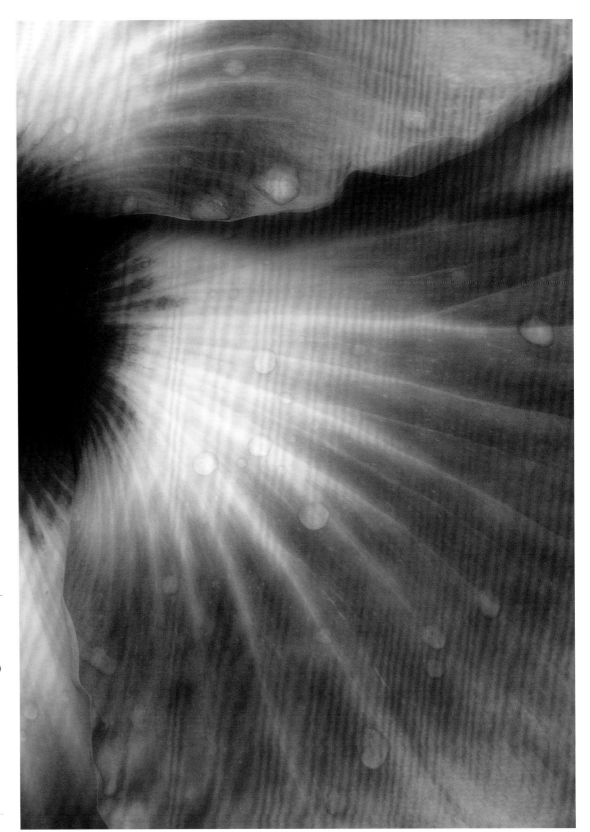

► **MICHAEL LOWE** FINALIST
Heavy Metal Hibiscus
Longwood Gardens, Pennsylvania,
USA.

This Japanese hibiscus (*Hibiscus rosa-sinensis*) is called 'Fifth Dimension' – what an apt description. Due to distracting background elements a 180mm macro lens was used to isolate a pleasing composition. The metallic look and colour were what initially attracted me to this flower, and the combination of the inorganic and organic makes this one of the most striking flowers in my opinion.

📷 **Canon EOS 5D**

◄ **LENA PESULA**   Highly commended
Colourful
Uppsala, Sweden.

This picture was taken in a botanical garden in southern Sweden, and I just love these colourful flowers. The more colours in a flower, the more I love them. Bees also adore the poppy (*Papaver*) and use them as an excellent pollen source. I wanted to capture the last, late summer colours and I found these poppies dancing in the wind – as if they were waving goodbye to the summer.

📷 **Canon EOS 30D, Canon 100mm macro**

► **NIKKI DE GRUCHY** FINALIST

Lotus

La Concepción Historical-Botanical Gardens, Malaga, Andalucia, Spain.

Nelumbo nucifera, an aquatic perennial, is known by a number of names, including 'sacred lotus'. The leaf surface exhibits a very high water-repellency and clever 'self-cleaning' mechanism, as seen by the spherical water droplet on the right which contains a tiny piece of plant material. I was struck by the blackness of the water in the lotus ponds, and how the flowers arose simply from the mud below it. This echoes Eastern symbolism: arising from the darkness is a growth of pure beauty. I made use of the diffused light from a cloudy day and selected an overhead position. This served both to highlight the shapes and to minimise reflections, capturing the dark water with the long stems of the lotus just visible, indicating the origins of the plant from an unknown depth.

📷 **Canon EOS 5D Mark I, 135mm f/2 L lens, f/6.3**

JULIA CLAXTON   Second
_____
Fruiting Bodies
Storrington, West Sussex, England.

Fungi are tentatively identified as sulphur tuft, amethyst deceiver, fly agaric, false chanterelle, olive brittlegill and wood blewit. The initial impetus for this work was the richness and diversity of form in the fruiting bodies of fungi, the sense of the hidden revealed in their sudden appearance. I also wanted tto portray something of the myths and mystery that traditionally surround them.

   An earlier fascination with photograms led me to experiment with making digital images using a scanner as a recording device or 'camera'. The actual fungi have been placed on the scanner and scanned, then arranged in Photoshop. They are then printed on fine art papers.

📷 **Umax Powerlook III Scanner**

1

2

1– Sulphur tuft (*Hypholoma fasciculare*)
2– Amethyst deceiver (*Laccaria amethystina*)

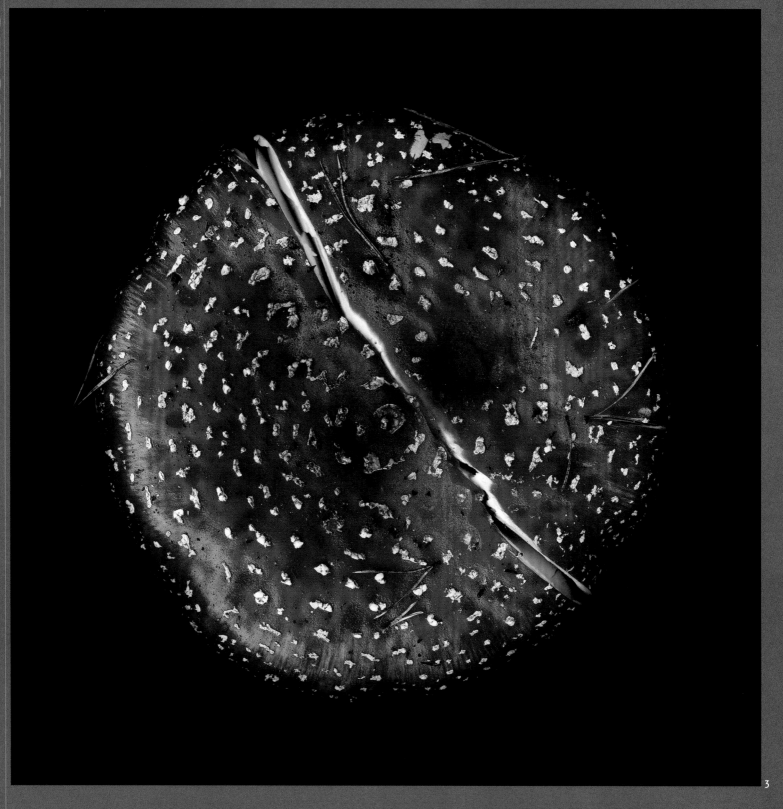

3

4

5

6

3– Fly agaric (*Amanita muscaria*)

4– False chanterelle (*Hygrophoropsis aurantiaca*)

5– Olive brittlegill (*Russula olivacea*)

6– Wood blewit (*Lepista nuda*)

▲ NIGEL SYMINGTON HIGHLY COMMENDED
Water Lilies
Ambalapuzha, Kerala, South India.

As the sun comes up a single water lily reaches above the surface of a mirror-smooth pond.
Its leaves form flat plates on the surface of the water. A large drop of dew has gathered in
the centre of one leaf, giving an impression of coolness before the heat of the day builds up.
A solitary green blade of grass provides a splash of contrast in an otherwise largely two-tone
image. I used a low camera angle to capitalise on the low rays of the rising sun. I explored the
best camera position to give a pleasing composition to the leaves, and bracketed the exposure to
achieve an optimum balance between the leaves, the water surface and the bloom.

📷 Nikon D700, Nikkor AF–S VR 70–200mm f/2.8G at 200mm, f/11

► CLAUDIA WASS HIGHLY COMMENDED
Calla Lily
Table top in my conservatory.

Warm-toned monochrome, grainy, fine art portrait of the bloom of a single white calla lily.
I wanted to create a fine art image that would accentuate the beauty and simplicity of the lily.

📷 Nikon D300, Sigma 105mm, f/2.8

◄ **JACKY PARKER**   <small>HIGHLY COMMENDED</small>
Soft Tones of Autumn
Buckinghamshire, England.

The soft white coneflowers (*Echinacea purpurea* 'White Lustre') in amongst the delicate soft grasses of *Stipa tenuissima*. I liked the way the soft grasses seemed to wrap themselves around the white coneflowers, gently swaying in the breeze.

📷 **Nikon D200, Nikkor 105 micro VR**

◄ STEPHEN STUDD FINALIST

Agave Red Spines Backlit

Jardin Majorelle, Marrakech, Morocco.

This image depicts the first rays of sunlight hitting the garden, highlighted from behind the red spines on this *Agave* plant. The sunlight from behind also shows the translucent leaves and gives the shadows an air of mystery, and I liked the patterns on the back of the leaf. I focused on part of the highlighted red spines, wanting to knock the rest out of focus. Exposing just for the red spines also pushes the rest of the image into shadow, apart from the translucent part of the leaf.

📷 **Canon EOS 1Ds Mark II, Canon 24–70mm, f/8**

▲ ANDY LATHAM FINALIST

***Polytrichum* Mounds**

Moor Piece Nature Reserve, near Clitheroe, Lancashire, England.

I had been commissioned by Lancashire Wildlife Trust to photograph the landscapes of their nature reserves. I was intrigued by this large group of mounds, more akin to boulders than mosses, and was fortunate to have some sunlight break through to add atmosphere. I wanted to show the spread of the moss within the surrounding landscape while also conveying something of the atmosphere and mystery of this peaceful nature reserve.

📷 **Velvia 50, Mamiya 7II, 65mm, f/22**

◄ **VICTOR KORCHENKO**　　　　　　　　　　　　　　　FIRST

Tai Chi

Beihai Park (imperial garden near Forbidden City), Beijing, China.

Every morning Beihai Park is filled with dozens of people performing various forms of traditional gymnastics and playing traditional music. This brings life to the thousand-year-old imperial garden and is probably its main feature.

Nikon D80

▲ GÖSTA LINDBOM   SECOND
Autumn Time in My Garden
Our garden.

Suddenly I saw him sitting there, tired yet relaxed, staying in the exact same position. It seemed such a striking image, so in that moment I took the photo.

📷 Kodachrome, Leica M2, Summicron 35mm, 1/50 sec, f/8

► LYNN KEDDIE   THIRD
'He Who Plants a Garden Plants Happiness'
Alf and Christine's garden in Stroud, Gloucestershire, England.

Alf had just harvested several varieties of different coloured carrots so that we could photograph them. Christine, his wife, came out to join us and they both walked back up the garden with their hands full of brightly coloured vegetables. They were obviously sharing a special moment, which is reflected in the cheeky grin on Christine's face. They seemed to be great friends and obviously respected and loved each other. We all worked well together, talking about their love of gardening and sharing tips. They were sharing a secret moment together when I clicked the shutter. Gardens are about people. This photograph just makes me smile.

📷 Canon 5D Mark II, Canon DF 200mm f/2.8L USM, f/8

▲ **JOHNNY JETSTREAM**   Highly commended

Versailles

Château de Versailles, Paris, France.

It's hard to imagine how the gardens at Versailles would have looked without people.
Presumably that's why there are so many statues lining the avenues. Many landscapes and
gardens are at their best without people, but Versailles thrives with the colour and bustle of
its visitors.

📷 **Olympus E-3, Olympus 35–200 f/2.0, f/5.6**

▲ **JOHNNY JETSTREAM**   FINALIST

Lawnmower Man

Potsdamer Platz, Berlin, Germany.

Many of the new buildings at Potsdamer Platz in Berlin have rooftop gardens. On this particular afternoon the gardener was out mowing the rooftop lawn. As cities become denser the gardens are becoming higher.

📷 **Olympus E–1, 150mm f/2.0, f/5.6**

◄ JOANNA CLEGG

Nature Girl

Outside our farmhouse, Morvah, near Penzance, Cornwall, England.

My eight-year-old daughter was admiring an elephant hawk-moth that had just hatched from its chrysalis. The moth was on some willowherb growing along the side of our house, its wings still a little crinkled. It was a very exciting moment.

📷 Pentax K10D, Sigma 105mm 1:2.8 DG Macro, f/2.8

▲ BRAD MAILER FINALIST

Running Girls

Chapman Valley, Geraldton, Western Australia.

I had taken my family on a day trip to our friend's farm to take some photos. They were having such fun, laughing and running through the wildflowers, that I couldn't help but take their photo to remember what a great day we had.

📷 Cannon EOS 450D, Tamron AF 70–300, f/11

◄ **STEVE SATUSHEK**   FINALIST

Girl in her Garden

Our garden, Bellingham, Washington, USA.

My daughter Mia was out in the garden one summer morning checking on her plants. She was holding some morning glory flowers of the Convolvulaceae family (*Ipomoea purpurea*). The out-of-focus flowers that can be seen are batchelor buttons and sweet peas. The vines are climbing on a wire trellis with a hummingbird outline. It is a brief moment in time, capturing the intimacy of childhood inquisitiveness and innocence.

📷 Fuji Velvia, Canon EOS 1, 70–200mm, f/8

▲ **ZEMFIRA BAKYYEVA**   HIGHLY COMMENDED

Elderly Woman in the Garden

Neighbour's dacha near the city of Kazan, Volga region, Russia.

This image was taken in Russia, where many elderly people work really hard to grow food in their summer gardens (often because their survival still depends on it), but they also find strength and time to grow flowers just for the beauty and joy of it. This woman is very fond of her gladioli: every flower has a stick for support, enough sunshine and space to grow, and a lot of the woman's care.

📷 Nikon D70, Nikkor 18–70mm f/3.5–4.5G at 52mm, f/4.2

▲ FIONA RUCK FINALIST

Roadside Gardeners

Busy highway in Miyazaki, Japan.

Illustrating that gardening can be done anywhere, a team of Japanese council workers lovingly plant seedlings along this busy highway in Miyazaki, Japan. Working as an organised team, the council workers meticulously enhance the beauty of a place that would often be forgotten and disregarded.

📷 Canon EOS 20D, Canon 16–35mm, f/4.5

➤ ANDREA JONES FINALIST

Dr Shirley Sherwood

Hinton Manor, Oxfordshire, England.

This is a portrait of renowned botanical art collector Dr Shirley Sherwood sitting on a stone bench seat beneath the large leaves of *Gunnera manicata*. Dr Sherwood is wearing a vivid pink hat with lime green jacket which contrasts with the green of the plant foliage.

📷 Kodak Pro SLR/n

◄ **DAVID LOW**   <small>HIGHLY COMMENDED</small>

Pathway to Glory

MacRitchie Reservoir, Singapore.

As we were strolling along the boardwalk the morning ray caught my attention and I thought how nice it would be if there was a silhouette subject ahead of us. As there were many other strollers and joggers around, I knew that it was just a matter of time before I would capture that moment. This couple offered me that opportunity.

📷 Panasonic FZ-50, Kit Lens 35–420mm, f/7.1

► **RICHARD BLOOM**   FINALIST

Head Gardener Fergus Garrett at Great Dixter Gardens

Great Dixter, East Sussex, England.
© Richard Bloom/National Magazines

This was shot for *Country Living* magazine as part of an ongoing series entitled 'The Passionate Gardener', which focuses on gardeners, horticulturists, plants people etc. and their individual horticultural passions. This particular feature was on Fergus Garrett and his tulips at Great Dixter.

   I could see the location would work well in black and white due to the varying textures of the wooden shed, thatched roof and grass in front, which would give the image a fairly broad tonal range. The structure of the shed also frames Fergus and centres the attention on him. The pot of tulips and bulb planter were relevant props for the story.

📷 Nikon D200

◄ **RICHARD BLOOM**   Highly commended

Peter Boardman

Peter Boardman, farmer and holly grower in his garden in Norfolk, England.

© Richard Bloom/National Magazines

This particular feature for *Country Living* was on Peter Boardman and his holly collection. Peter is sitting on a bench set within half a salvaged upturned boat in his garden trimming stems of holly. I needed to portray Peter within the context of his holly collection at How Hill Farm, Norfolk, hence the crate of holly trimmings. The upturned boat was perfect, both in terms of how it would look in black and white and how it would frame the subject.

📷 Nikon D200

► **GILLIAN HUNT**

Camouflage

My garden.

The subject is a brightly coloured chaffinch, camouflaged amongst equally bright sycamore buds and the subtle colour of the lichen. The light, the colour, the luck – a bird landing amongst the buds I was photographing, whose colour reflected that of the buds and the lichen. What were the chances? The whole set-up had a soft focus, circular frame of branches, which draws the eye in to the subject. How could I resist this shot?

I only had seconds to take the picture as the bird landed on the tree where I was photographing the sycamore buds. I had to quickly re-frame, focus and click, and luckily I managed to take three shots before he had gone again. Right place, right time, quick thinking.

📷 **Nikon D2X, Nikon 70–200 f/2.8**

◄ **MAGDALENA WASICZEK**   S<small>ECOND</small>

Mimikra

Trzebinia, Malopolska region, Poland.

I was playing with the composition of a still life with pears when I saw this peacock butterfly nestling amongst the fruit. Beautiful and brightly coloured, its wings provided excellent camouflage.

📷 Nikon D300, Tamron 90, f/6.3, 1/160sec, ISO320, +0,3EV

▲ **JACKY PARKER**   T<small>HIRD</small>

Crabby

Buckinghamshire, England.

A little crab spider (*Misumena vatia*) waiting to ambush prey amongst the petals of a shasta daisy (*Leucanthemum × superbum*).

📷 Nikon D300, Nikkor 105 micro VR

▲ **VALERIE McANINCH**

Early Morning Cardinal
Backyard, Springfield, Ohio, USA.

I started shooting wildlife seriously about four years ago and I am fascinated by Audubon prints. This is a photograph of a male cardinal. It took me weeks to photograph the pair, which I spotted in an area outside my office window that I had set up for shooting in the winter. I considered removing the screen from the window, but I found that I liked the diffused filter effect I got from shooting through the glass with the screen.

📷 Canon Digital Rebel, Canon EF 300mm 1:4, f/4

► **DAVID CHAPMAN**

Great Spotted Woodpecker (*Dendrocopos major*)
My garden in Townshend, Cornwall, England.

I had enjoyed watching the woodpeckers feeding on peanuts in the garden and wanted to capture a portrait of them. I particularly liked the way the backlighting created a rim-lighting on the birds. I had been feeding the birds, including the woodpeckers, in the garden. This female had eaten and hopped up the branch of the tree to drum. I used a hide to conceal myself so that I could capture the right shot.

📷 Canon 5D Mark 2, 800mm, f/6.3

◄ J. KEITH BERGER   FINALIST
Bigger Than Life
Backyard vegetable garden, Sacramento, California, USA.

Mantises do not actively hunt their prey. They usually stay hidden or
camouflaged, waiting, unmoving and virtually invisible on a leaf or stem,
poised to seize any passing insect. This tiny but tenacious young mantis
seems to be practising a new technique, perhaps for scaring away other
predators, perched in full sight, casting a shadow much more imposing than
its actual size.

   There are so many layers of life in a garden. We're often inspired by the
brilliance of a blossom or the graceful arc of a leaf in sunshine or in shadow.
But I also like to look more deeply, finding inspiration in the small but
significant life forms that are less visible at first glance.

📷 **Kodak Z712 IS**

▲ TECK PING TONG   FINALIST
Sweet Lovers
My backyard garden.

In the original image there are three insects, with two meeting each other
and the other one looking on. I tried to present them from a more romantic
point of view, so I cropped out the onlooker at extreme right. These insects
are thin and long-legged, with yellow with black lines, and are about 10mm
in height. They like decayed papayas and are very timid. Familiar with their
behaviour, I prepared the necessary gear and, after some hard sweat one
morning, managed to snap a few good shots.

📷 **Sony Alpha 100, Minolta Macro 100mm 2.8, f/6.3**

▲ RACHEL PIPER   FINALIST

Frog in my Garden

A makeshift pond in my garden.

This handsome frog was photographed in a makeshift pond in my garden. It was a very obliging frog, which posed beautifully for the camera. It didn't seem to mind how close I got, and I was able to capture the texture of its skin and the patterns on its face in perfect detail. Its home was only very small, but it seemed happy to wallow in the water and look into my lens. In the spring of 2009 I decided to observe the amazing transformation of tadpoles into frogs, photographing each stage of their development. This one seemed to invite me to take a photograph, posing beautifully for the camera. How could I resist?

📷 **Nikon Coolpix P90, f/8**

▲ FENCE MATE

Night-time hunters

Hungary.

I live in the Hungarian 'puszta' on a farm. Over the last few years I have installed a lot of bird dens in nearby trees in which rollers, kestrels, starlings and the long-eared owl family in the picture nest each year. The chicks leave the nest two weeks before they can fly and beg for food from their parents throughout the night. Sometimes their hooting is so loud that it wakes me up! These birds are used to our presence and the young ones can be photographed easily during the day. The special feature of this picture is the long, 10-second exposure, which was enough to make a few stars in the sky clearly seen. The birds were lit by flash.

📷 **Nikon D300, 20mm, f/16, 1/10 sec**

◄ RAOUL SLATER Highly Commended
Birdbath
Our front yard, Pomona, Sunshine Coast, Queensland, Australia.

We made this birdbath from a section of old water pipe and placed it carefully so that the sun would backlight it in winter – our dry season, when birds visit most regularly. The mosaic took three years to complete and shows our cat Oscar (now sadly departed), chooks and one of the resident blue-faced honeyeaters.

📷 **Canon EOS 30D, 75–300mm, f/5, 1/64 sec**

▲ PAUL MIGUEL Highly Commended
Long Tailed Tit in Snowstorm
Woodland edge, organic farm, Swillington, West Yorkshire, England.

The long tailed tit (*Aegithalos caudatus*) is a bird that often visits gardens in small flocks during the winter.

I wanted to create an atmospheric image that depicted a typical garden visitor braving extreme conditions. Rather than just photograph the snowy backdrop, I wanted to record the snowflakes falling around the bird to convey the mood. During a period of heavy snowfall, I got into my hide in order to capture this wintry image. With a neutral background, I chose a brightly coloured dogwood stem to add a splash of colour, and used a rating of ISO 400 to obtain a fast shutter speed.

📷 **Canon EOS 20D, Canon f/4 300mm with 1.4x converter, f/5.6**

◄ MAGDALENA WASICZEK   FINALIST

When the Day Ends

Trzebinia, Malopolska region, Poland.

I love the peace and quiet of the summer evening. I long to sit and soak up the smells and sounds of the meadows. Around me are fading lanterns of dandelions, and sleeping insects on each blade of grass. It was the last picture of the day and I had to capture, out of the darkness, the tiny butterfly, a brown argus (*Aricia agestis*) against the sow thistle (*Sonchus oleraceus*).

📷 **Nikon D300, Tessar 50/2.8, f/2.8, 1/500sec, ISO 400**

▲ STEPHEN DOGGETT   HIGHLY COMMENDED

The Prey's View

Taree, around 300km north of Sydney, Australia.

This is a close-up of the head and palps of a male spider belonging to the genus *Dinopis*, commonly called the 'ogre-faced' or 'net caster' spider. It was photographed against a brick wall, hence the orange hue.

Dinopis spiders are quite common around Sydney. They hunt by hanging upside down holding a small web net. When prey walks past the spider leaps onto the creature and wraps it up in the net before dispatching it with a venomous kiss.

This spider was sitting on brick-work at a height – almost out of arm's reach. Fortunately, it was possible (via stretching and live view on the camera) to compose and focus the shot. The high magnification, with the very narrow depth of field, and the awkward position meant that achieving focus was challenging. The submitted image was the only shot on the day that I managed to successfully capture!

📷 **Canon 50D, Canon MPE65, f/16**

This was taken at around 4x magnification hand held with the MPE65 and the MT24ex flash. I was able to stabilise the camera by resting it on the brickwork below the spider.

▲ DIRK HECKMANN

Squirrel with Nut

Tree in the Botanical Garden of Berlin, Germany.

I was watching the squirrels in the Botanical Garden in Berlin for quite some time. When I saw which way they went up and down the trees, I put myself directly under the tree to look up the trunk to capture the perfect shot.

📷 Canon 40D, 70–200mm, f/2.8

► COLIN VARNDELL

Greenfinches

My garden in Netherbury, Dorset, England.

I arranged a portable hide near a peanut basket on a cold day, and sat in it with my camera on a tripod focused just off the peanuts. As the two arguing male greenfinches hovered nearby, I tripped the shutter.

📷 Nikon D300, 500mm, f/8, ISO 800, 1/1250 sec

THE EDIBLE GARDEN

▲ **MARK BOLTON**   FIRST

Autumn Morning Down on the Allotments
Alderman Moore's Allotments, Bristol, England.

This photograph was taken on an autumn morning, complete with mists and a lot of 'mellow fruitfulness'. The location was on the allotments in the centre of Bristol, and I was probably walking towards my own site thinking about what I was about to pick!

📷 **Canon G9**
Hand-held, probably used my hand to screen the lens from flare.

▲ **CAROL SHARP**

Heritage Purple Podded Pea

Studio.

I grew these purple podded peas from seeds from Garden Organic's Heritage Seed Library, as part of a self-initiated project to find beautiful and garden-worthy heritage vegetable varieties from their library. The seeds are being saved for our future biodiversity – they are our heirlooms. This was my favourite. The plant was attractive in all its stages, from flower to seed pod. I painted the background and composed the shot to evoke the mood of an old master's still life painting.

   Pisum sativum 'Purple Podded' is a heritage variety supplied by Garden Organic. This is a great garden worthy plant with beautiful bicolour burgundy and pink flowers, followed by the rich burgundy pods, mottling with green as they ripen.

📷 **Leaf Aptus 65 back on a Sinar 5x4 camera, 150mm**

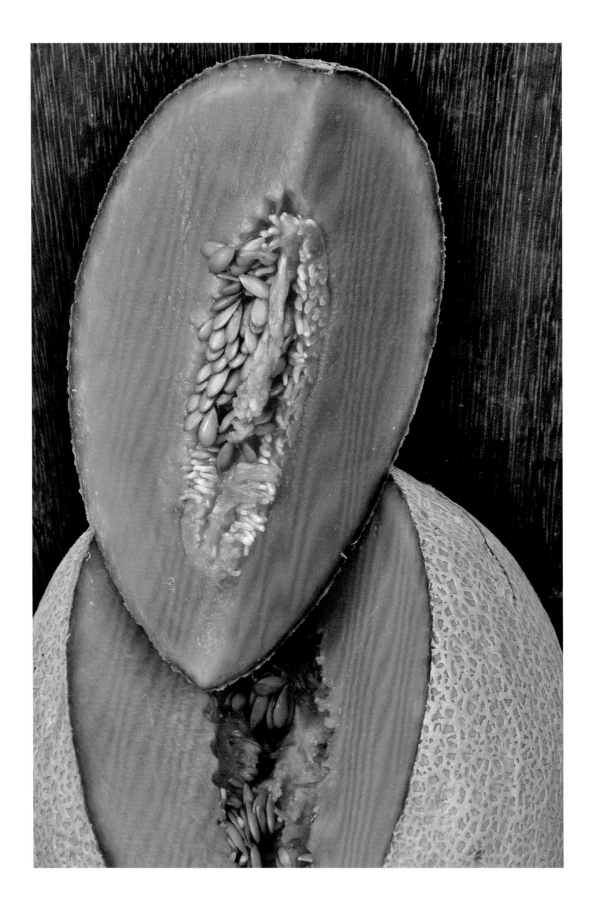

◄ **CARLO SILVA** THIRD

Melone Modigliani

Lombardy, Italy.

This is an interpretation of a natural product – an example of one of many original and particular gifts of the earth. The shot is inspired by Jeanne Hébuterne in a painting by Amedeo Modigliani.

📷 **Nikon D200, Nikkor 18–200 VR F 13**

▲ **ANNE GILBERT** HIGHLY COMMENDED

Fresh Fruit Salad

Home studio, England.

English fruit, herbs and red watercress all combined to make a 'blooming' floral platter. Not only were the components all beautifully decorative, it smelt great and I got to cook and eat with them later on too!

📷 **Nikon D300, 17–55mm f/2.8, f/11**

► **RICHARD BLOOM**   HIGHLY COMMENDED

Figs

Table within my home.

Two and a half figs on a table. A simple and rustic-looking still life showing both the form and rich colour of the fruit as well as the intricate internal structure.

Figs are beautiful, natural objects, both to look at and to touch. The simple satisfying form and rich deep purple colour are enough on their own, but when sliced open they reveal this wonderfully intricate internal structure. I wanted to photograph these qualities in as simple and unfussy a way as possible.

Nikon D200

◄ **RICHARD BLOOM** FINALIST
Rhubarb
Bressingham, Norfolk, England.

Freshly picked rhubarb from my grandfather's rhubarb patch (in fact this variety is called 'Grandad's Favourite') in a wooden trug surrounded by dandelion flowers.

I had been harvesting some of the crop to take home and noticed a meadow close by that was covered with dandelion flowers, which I could see would contrast well with the deep pink stems of the rhubarb.

📷 Nikon D200

► **SERGEY KAREPANOV** <small>HIGHLY COMMENDED</small>
Russian Strawberries
Brolino forest garden, near Moscow, Russia.

In the shadows of the colossal pines in the Russian forest garden wild strawberries grow. You cannot see the tiny red berries when you are walking by, as the plants are only 7cm tall.

📷 **Canon EOS 1 Ds Mark III, Canon EF 100 mm f/2.8 Macro USM**

◄ **DEBORAH CASSO**   Highly commended

Green Tomato Abstract

My backyard garden, Seattle, Washington, USA.

The soft form of the green tomato caught my eye.
The background shades of green in the late summer
garden and the shallow depth of field helped to simplify
the composition.

📷 Nikon D200, Nikkor 105mm macro, f/4.0

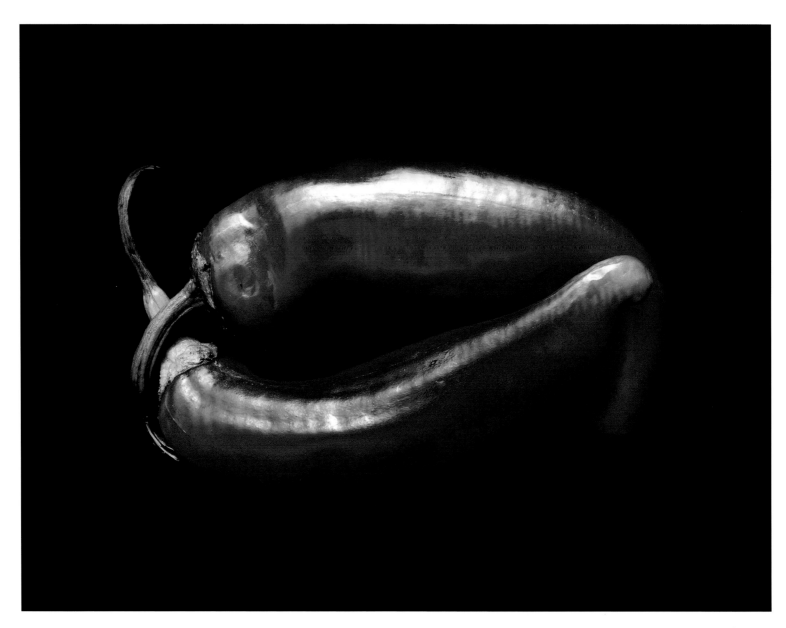

▲ GIOIA ALOISI AND MONICA GORINI   HIGHLY COMMENDED

Lovers

Personal photographic studio.

We discovered these peppers in a box at the market. Their human form stood out, so we took them into the studio to photograph. We were amazed by the delicacy of this embrace. The two peppers representing the emotion of human love.

📷 **Nikon camera**

► CAROLINE HYMAN   FINALIST

Pomegranates

Home studio, England.

This image forms part of a series of still lifes featuring fruit and vegetables. The colour and shape of pomegranates has always intrigued me, and I had always wanted to photograph them.

📷 **Ilford HP5, Hasselblad 501c, Planar f/2.8 80m**

Sepia-toned and hand-coloured silver bromide print.

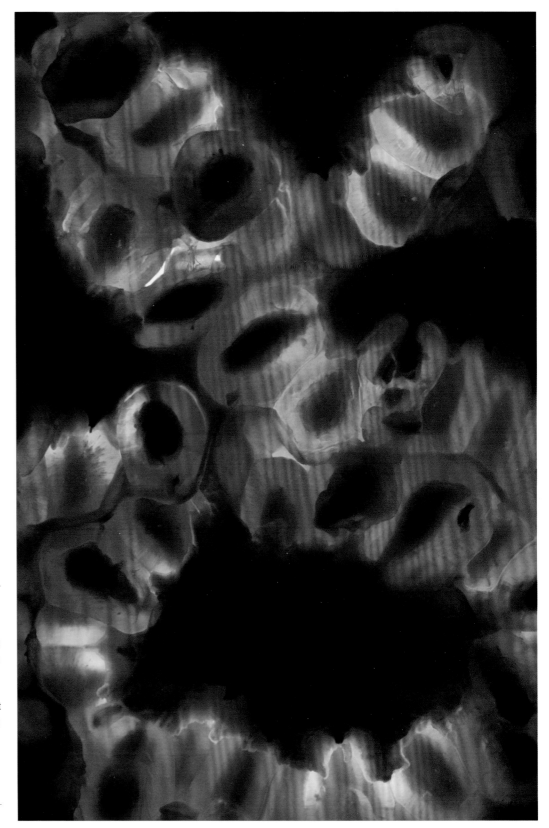

► **PETER KARRY**   HIGHLY COMMENDED

Patterns in a Pomegranate
Home studio.

Having enjoyed photographing translucent items backlit on top of my lightbox, I was inspired to experiment with fruit. Having seen oranges shot this way I felt that a pomegranate might benefit from similar treatment.

   I started by buying several pomegranate fruits so that I could cut them up and have several thin slices, starting through the centre. I then made sure that the slice to be shot was as level as possible and used a tripod and remote release to keep the camera still – light levels being low.

📷 **Sony Alpha A700, Tamron 90mm f/2.8 macro, f/16**

◀ **CAROLE DRAKE**   FINALIST

Tendril

Dorset, England.

I took lots of photographs of the tendrils of sugar snap peas clasping onto fine plastic netting in my vegetable garden and this was one of the simplest. I like the way that it's stripped down to the essentials, so simple that it could be a drawing. I interpreted it as a monochrome image to emphasise that parallel. It looks as if it could be a graphite drawing.

📷 **Nikon D200, Nikon 105mm macro**

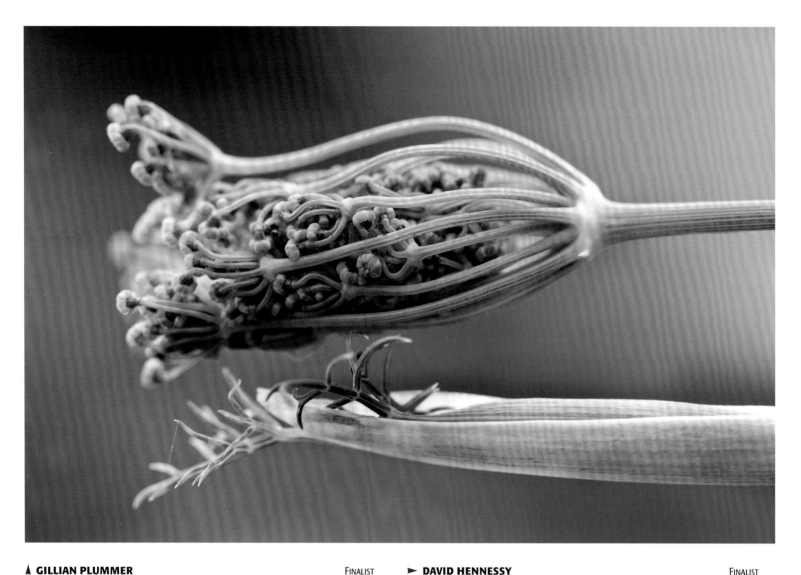

▲ GILLIAN PLUMMER   FINALIST

Fennel Fiesta

My garden in Suffolk, England.

I was attracted by the bronze colour of the stems and then fascinated by all the detail, and just had to capture it. I got up early several mornings running, as the sun shifted around it. My intention was to capture the detail locked inside the stems, but the boldness of the stems themselves took over.

📷 **Canon Mark V, Canon 100mm macro, f/5.6**

► DAVID HENNESSY   FINALIST

Autumn Harvest

Narborough Hall, Narborough, Norfolk, England.

I wanted to show the shapes and colours of the apple varieties grown at Narborough Hall. The rich redness of the hanging chillies and the soft texture of the roses complemented the display of fruit. The dried flowers evoke the transition from summer to autumn. Displayed to show their dimension and colours, a variety of apples were arranged on a steel blue slate base set against a background of a 'ring of fire' of chilli peppers and an earthenware vase filled with dried flowers.

📷 **Nikon D 200, Nikon DX 18–200, f/16**

▲ **JOHN ROGER PALMOUR**   FIRST

Harvesting the Vegetable Garden

Suches, Union County, Georgia, USA.

My wife and I were exploring the back roads of North Georgia one July morning. As we stopped
at this small farm, with a rooster crowing in the background, the lady arrived in her pickup
with her two dogs and began harvesting the squash, peppers, tomatoes, green beans and
corn. The early morning lighting, the general atmosphere, with mists rising from overnight
thundershowers, created an incredible scene. It was one of those pictures that seem to take
themselves.

📷 **Nikon D40, Nikon 18–55mm, f/7.1**

I did not have time to use a tripod, and shot on the 'auto' setting.

▲ **ANDREA JONES** <small>SECOND</small>

Pennsylvania in Winter with Covering of Frost

The Caryopteris Allee, Longwood Gardens, Pennsylvania, USA.

The beautiful contrast of shapes and forms includes evergreen hedging and topiary, a classical temple, urn and plinth, frost, and dried *Caryopteris* foliage. The subdued colour range and the frost adds a sparkle to the shot.

📷 **Kodak DCS Pro SLR/n**

▼ **CATHERINE SPRATT** <small>THIRD</small>

At the Bottom of the Garden

North Topsail Beach, North Carolina, USA.

Last October, we were staying with friends, Jim and Garry, at their beach house in North Topsail Beach. After our visit they would shut the house as they had no more rentals booked until Christmas. The previous day's weather had been glorious but this morning we could see the approach of winter.

📷 **Nikon D70, Nikkor AF-S 18–70mm, f/10**

◄ **COLIN ROBERTS** FIRST

Tree-Lined Landscape
Southern England.

Trees in a stretch of rolling English landscape, photographed at first light in spring. The trees follow the hedge-lines between the fields, decorating the landscape with their rounded shapes. The misty atmosphere diminishes the tones of the most distant trees, helping to convey a feeling of depth in the scene.

📷 **Canon 1Ds Mark II, 135mm, f/16**

I used a 0.6 ND filter to control contrast, and a polarizer to enhance the colours.

▲ TOM WUNDRAK

SECOND

Autumn Melody

Franconia, Germany.

It was the poetical and abstract quality of this view up into the autumnal sky which inspired me to take this photograph. The leaves resemble a musical score writing a melody of autumn. Finding the right layout for all the elements – the close-up foliage and the distant silhouettes of the trees – was the main task here as I wanted to achieve an asymmetrical, well-balanced composition from a particular perspective.

📷 **Nikon D70, Nikkor 2.8 20–35mm, f/9**

► CHINCH GRYNIEWICZ

THIRD

New Growth

Pembrokeshire, Wales.

I was inspired by the graceful fragility of the leaves, emphasised by the delicate light on them, but counterpointed by the jagged serration of the leaf margins. I also very much enjoyed how the compositional weight of the large and small 'set' of leaves complemented each other. I intensified the translucent quality of the leaves by adding fill-in flash from behind. Photographing against a white background brings out the essence of this picture – simplicity and purity.

📷 **Fuji Finepix S3Pro, Nikon 24-85mm f/2.8-4 (at 85mm), f/22**
Fill-in flash from behind, white background, longish exposure (1.5 seconds)

JANE GREGORY   FINALIST

Bonsai Trees
Home studio.

I collect and record botanical specimens, in this case whole bonsai trees. I manipulate the images, enjoying the ambiguity of scale, colour and structure that the specimens suggest.

These images are made using a flatbed scanner in a process echoing Victorian activities, such as flower pressing and botanical illustration. The bonsai trees were captured digitally and quite heavily manipulated in Photoshop. Whole trees are dissected and reassembled; elements are grafted and cloned; colours are modified. The resultant images are ambiguous in scale, structure and authenticity.

I'm fascinated by Victorian botanical illustration and the desire to systematically catalogue species. Here, I have concentrated on bonsai, the practice of cultivating small trees that mimic the shape and style of mature, full-sized trees. I have particularly enjoyed playing with the ambiguity of scale and the potential to digitally create fictional, imagined trees.

📷 **Flatbed scanner**

1– Crimson Yew
2– Yellow Pepper
3– Yellow Ash
4– Red Elm
5– Orange Mandarin
6– Amber Serissa

1

2

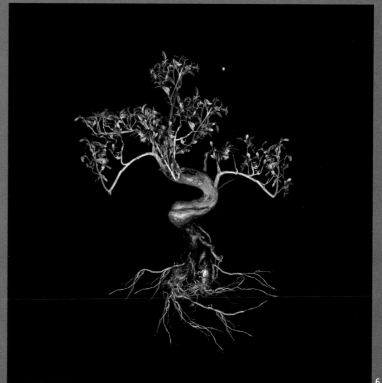

▲ **MICHAEL SCHLEGEL**   Hɪɢʜʟʏ ᴄᴏᴍᴍᴇɴᴅᴇᴅ

The Gate
Freiburg, Germany.

This is a view of a small path leading through two trees on a foggy autumn morning. This place is just outside my hometown of Freiburg, and I frequently drive by them. My photography is often done in foggy conditions, and on this particular morning the conditions and light were perfect, resulting in this dark and surreal atmosphere.

📷 **Canon EOS 400D**

▲ **MICHAEL LOWE**　　　　　　　　　　　　　　　　Highly commended

Smoky Mountains

Shenandoah National Park, Virginia, USA.

Remnants of fast-moving clouds give the illusion of smoke rising from the tree-covered
mountainside. This shot is actually taken looking down at the opposite mountain. Although it
wasn't taken in the Great Smoky Mountains of North Carolina and Tennessee, I felt that this
image gave me the feel of being there.

📷 **Canon EOS 5D Mark II**

◄ **SHOKOUFEH MALEKKIANI**   HIGHLY COMMENDED

Bujan

Bujan, Iran.

This was a small village located in a valley surrounded by aspen trees, fruit trees, plane trees and old walnut trees. I wanted to portray industrial living beside pure nature, and try to show that we can use technology, such as road construction, at the same time as protecting the environment.

📷 Canon EOS 5D, EF 70–200 F 2.8L USM, f/2.8

◄ HOWARD LITHERLAND FINALIST

The Essence of the Wood

Gwysanney Drive, near Mold, Wales.

I was drawn to the delicate quality of the light playing on the pine trunks as the sun set, revealing a soft, dreamlike quality to the trees and grasses. Concentrating on just the trunks and intentionally moving the camera during the shot blurred fine detail and revealed the trees' colour and texture. This technique echoes impressionist art, of which I am very fond.

📷 **Canon 5D, 24–105mm (at 105mm) f/16**

▲ ELEANOR SCRIVEN HIGHLY COMMENDED

The Lone Tree

Winnat's Pass, Castleton, Derbyshire, England.

Winter sun highlights a lone tree standing atop the towering crags of Winnats Pass, near Castleton in the Derbyshire Peak District, on a frosty February morning. Winnats means 'wind gates', and sometimes the wind in the pass seems to blow at you from every direction. On this particular day, however, the stillness was almost eerie, the silence only broken by the occasional bleating of the resident sheep.

📷 **Canon EOS 400D, Canon 18–55mm kit lens, f/10**

ANNEMARIE FARLEY HIGHLY COMMENDED

A Colourful Celebration of Leaves

Stanley Park, Blackpool, England.

Autumn has always been my favourite time of year, purely because the leaves on the trees are an amazing colour. In this selection of leaves I wanted to show and celebrate these vibrant colours. I used two leaves for each of the finished images; I felt that the texture and colour of each leaf was so individual (almost like the palm of the hand) that I used a different leaf to provide an interesting and unique background, highlighting every mark, pattern and scar that each leaf displays.

📷 **Nikon D300, Nikon 18–55mm, f/16**

1– Maidenhair tree (*Ginkgo biloba*)

2– Rowan or mountain ash (*Sorbus aucuparia*)

3– Hawthorn (*Crataegus monogyna*)

4– Pedunculate oak (*Quercus robur*)

5– Cherry Plum (*Prunus cerasifera* var. *atropurpurea*)

6– Field Maple (*Acer campestre*)

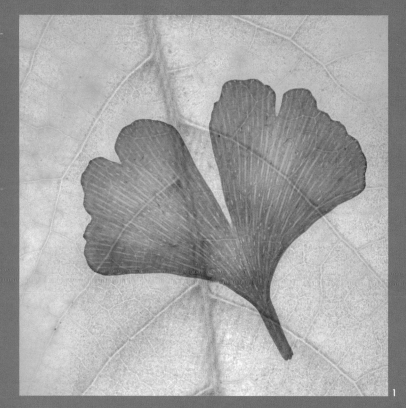

1

2

▲ OLEGAS KURASOVAS   FINALIST

Leaf Fall at Forest Stream

Dukshtos, Lithuania.

This was taken in early October at a small forest stream in Lithuania. The variety of autumnal colours is a beautiful subject to shoot, and although this place has a special aura all year round, it reveals its best colours in autumn. I used a tripod while I stood in cold water, and after a few moments took this picture.

📷 **Canon 20D, Tokina 12–24mm, f/16**

► COLIN ROBERTS   HIGHLY COMMENDED

Pinewoods in Mist

New Forest National Park, Hampshire, England.

This shot reveals a sapling reaching for the light in the New Forest National Park, photographed in a thick mist with autumn tints in the grasses and bracken. I liked the contrast of scale between the young sapling growing among the grasses and the towering trunks of the mature trees around it. The tall trees appear like guardians. The position of this solitary sapling in a mature plantation sparked an idea, so I chose my viewpoint carefully and used a telephoto lens to help isolate the young tree against a backdrop of tall trunks in a forest plantation of Corsican pines.

📷 **Canon 1Ds Mark II, 135mm, f/16**

I used a 0.3 ND filter to control contrast, and a polarizer to enhance the colours.

◄ **HELEN ASHTON**   FINALIST

Spooky Woods 2

Longridge Fell, Lancashire, England.

This fell is constantly changing – every time I walk up here the landscape is different, so this shot may never be replicated. With the light and the feel of the woods, I felt as if I were in a secret place, never sure of what could step out from behind a tree.

📷 **Canon 5D, Canon 24–105, f/4**

▲ **JONATHAN LITTLE**   FINALIST

Autumn Reflection

Loch Chon, Stirlingshire, Scotland.

En route to a photographic weekend near Loch Lomond I spotted this small loch through a gap in the trees. The dull light only served to emphasise the vivid autumn colours along the shoreline, and their perfect mirrored reflection in the water. Five minutes later the heavens opened, and the perfect symmetry of the moment was gone.

📷 **Fuji Provia 120 roll film, Pentax 645NII, Pentax 33–55mm**

0.6ND Grad filter reversed to hold down reflections on the water.

MARCIN STAWIARZ   FINALIST

Portraits of Trees

Berkshire, England.

This is a series of photographs that I worked on for several months. Each picture required the relevant conditions, such as the setting sun, strong wind, and at the same time heavily overcast sky. In combination with a long exposure and infrared filter, I tried to create an image of trees which, for me, have souls, and often their shapes remind me of human silhouettes.

📷 **Canon 5D Mark II, Canon 17–40L, f/5.6 to f/8**
Every photo was made with an IR filter, with a long exposure of 240–360 seconds, and during strong wind.

► **PHILIP COLEMAN**   HIGHLY COMMENDED

Fall at Olive Lake, Oregon

Olive Lake, in eastern Oregon near town of Granite, USA.

The innkeeper had urged me to drive far along a gravel road and see Olive Lake in the mountains of eastern Oregon. It was a quiet, mostly cloudy October day. The colours of the mountain larch and evergreens glowed, beautifully mirrored in the calm lake surface. The gold in the leaves of the larch was spectacular.

📷 Nikon D300, Nikkor AF-S 70–300 DX VR (at 75 mm) f/8, ISO 320, 1/50 sec

JEAN MACDONALD HIGHLY COMMENDED

Trees and Sunrays in Forests in South Shropshire
Woodland surrounding Craven Arms in Shropshire, England.

📷 Canon EOS 20D and Canon EOS 30D, Canon EF 24–105mm f/4 L IS USM, f/3.5 through to f/8

▲ **REBECCA NEX**   FINALIST

The Whitewashed Tree
Chatsworth House, Derbyshire, England.

I saw this tree in the orangery in Chatsworth House, Derbyshire, growing against a whitewashed wall behind huge glass panes. The tree appears to have been whitewashed along with the wall, so the only colour is provided by these three leaves, creating a crucial focal point. I love the subtlety of the scene and the way that the whitewashing has literally stripped the tree of its colour, emphasising its delicate shape and pattern. Our family visits Chatsworth often, so this picture has an important emotional connection for me.

📷 **Canon 30D, Canon EF 75–300, f/13**

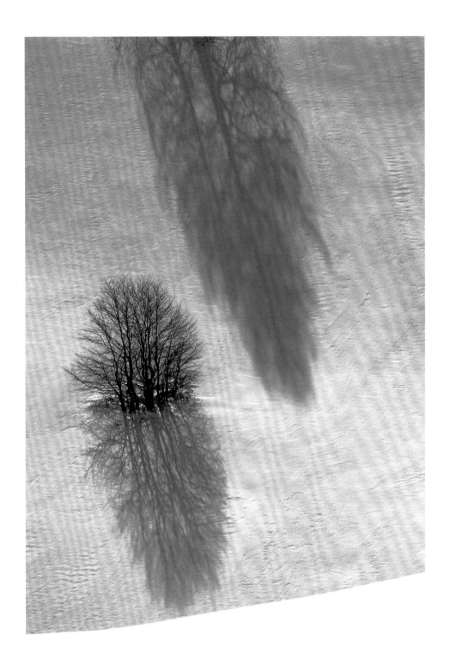

▲ **ARMANDO MANICIATI**

Shadows on the Snow

Monte Grappa, Veneto, Italy.

This image is based on contrasts in the white snow and the shadows. I tried to play with the diagonal lines of the shadows. There is a beech bush, and the big shadow is from a larch. I noticed the play of light and shade, and I composed this image with a medium telephoto lens.

📷 Fujichrome Velvia 50, Nikon F E2, Nikkor AF 300 f/4 IF-ED

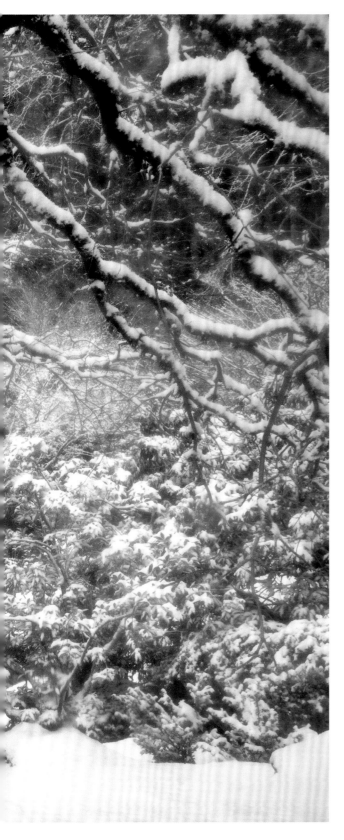

YOUNG GARDEN
PHOTOGRAPHER
OF THE YEAR

MATTHEW TAUZER

◄ **MATTHEW TAUZER – AGED 15**   First *Garden Views*

Snowfall in Eden

Portland Japanese Gardens, Portland, Oregon, USA.

In Portland, Oregon, snow is somewhat uncommon. In the morning I noticed snowflakes and decided to visit the most beautiful place I know: the Portland Japanese Gardens. The mixture of rare Portland snow and the beautiful landscaping of these gardens inspired me to capture something different and unique.

📷 Canon EOS Digital Rebel Xt, Canon EF 17–40mm f/4 L USM

▲ JONAH SURKES – AGED 12　　　　　SECOND *PEOPLE IN THE GARDEN*

Goal!!

My garden, at the end by our new goal.

My brother and I decided to do an action-shot session of him saving some footballs in the goal in our garden. I kicked the football at him and with my remote, I fired the shutter as he tried to make a save. We spent about two hours until we got the perfect timing and pose.

📷 **Nikon D70, Sigma 55–200mm**

► SAM CAIRNS – AGED 14　　　　　THIRD *WILDLIFE IN THE GARDEN*

Silhouetted Crested Tit

In my garden.

One day, out of my bedroom window, I saw a crested tit perched on this perch. I could see the potential of the image, so I began to feed it peanuts. When the weather was nice it became backlit and looked spectacular. Crested tits are an iconic species and they have a certain 'hairstyle' which distinguishes them from other birds. I prepared for a week before finding the brilliant weather conditions to create this shot.

📷 **Canon 10D, Canon EF 300mm f/2.8 IS USM, 1/800 sec**

▲ **BETH DEBOIS – AGED 15**

Bay Tree Shadow on a White Stone Wall

Local park, West London, England.

We were walking in our local park on a bright, sunny day in winter, looking for colours and shapes as there are not many flowers about that time of year. I liked the shadow of the bay tree (*Laurus nobilis*) because it was so simple.

▲ **ELEANOR EASTON – AGED 15**   Highly commended *Trees*

Watersmeet

Watersmeet National Trust Property, North Devon, England.
By kind permisssion of the National Trust.

I was inspired by the filigree of interlacing branches and the tall, slim trunks in the soft sunlight. I was on holiday in Devon and walking with my family through the National Trust property when the trees first caught my eye. I framed the photograph so that it was filled with the trees, cutting out the river, the sky and the ground, so there were no distractions; I wanted the picture to be all about the trees.

📷 Fujifilm Finepix S5700

▲ **MATTHEW TAUZER – AGED 15**   HIGHLY COMMENDED *GARDEN VIEWS*

Eden I

Portland Japanese Gardens, Portland, Oregon, USA.

This striking Japanese maple tree overlooking the upper pond was captured in the Strolling Pond Garden at the Portland Japanese Gardens, Portland. It's difficult to catch this tree in its peak autumn colours, so I was ecstatic to find that its autumnal foliage was this thick and brightly coloured. You can just see the garden's Moon Bridge in the background, as well as sculptures of crane (a Japanese symbol of longevity) towards the right.

📷 **Canon EOS Digital Rebel Xt, Canon EF 17–40mm f/4.0 L USM, f/7.1**

▲ **SAMUEL BAYLIS – AGED 15**   FINALIST *GARDEN VIEWS*

Autumn Reflections

Sheffield Park in Sussex, England.
By kind permisssion of the National Trust.

A lake with autumn-coloured trees around the edges reflected in the water. Sheffield Park house is visible in the background and there are three ducks swimming in the foreground.
I found a part of the lake where the view of the autumn colour and its reflection in the lake was particularly good. I then had to wait for the three ducks to swim in the right direction.

📷 Nikon D40, 8–55mm, f/6.3

▲ **JAMES HARKIN – AGED 15**   Highly Commended *Wildlife in the Garden*

The Final Apple

My back garden in Yarm, Teeside, England.

I love the contrast between the black of the blackbird and the white, cloudy winter sky. I feel the image portrays the harshness of January and how something will always live on – even through winter. After taking the silhouette I converted it to black and white to emphasise the darkness of the blackbird against the white of a cloudy winter's sky.

📷 **Canon EOS 30D, 100–300mm, f/11**

► **CHRISTIAN MAROT – AGED 15**   Highly Commended *People in the Garden*

Garden Night in France

France.

We built a camp fire at the end of our garden with the moon and the surrounding trees creating a spooky atmosphere. It contrasted with the warm glow the fire gave out, highlighting the sunflowers and my Dad.

📷 **Nikon D80, Nikon DX 18–105mm**

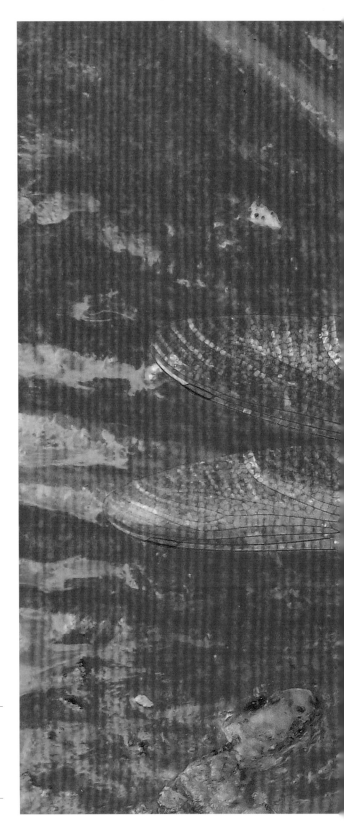

► **ZERINA KAPS – AGED 11**   FINALIST *WILDLIFE IN THE GARDEN*

Dragonfly on a Pumpkin
I took this photo at the terrace of my house.

I was inspired by the contrast of the red pumpkin and the green dragonfly. I saw the dragonfly on the pumpkin and there just happened to be a camera beside me on the table. Cautiously, I took a few pictures of the dragonfly.

📷 **Kodak Easyshare C743, 18mm, f/4.8**

◄ **JAMIE UNWIN – AGED 15**

◄ **JAMIE UNWIN – AGED 15**   FINALIST *WILDLIFE IN THE GARDEN*
Winter Robin
My front garden, Oxfordshire, England.

With a white blanket draped over the surrounding countryside and my front garden and house covered by a sweeping carpet of snow, I was eager to take some photos of the effects it had on the wildlife in my garden. I found this robin standing proudly in the crisp snow, and the way its red chest and the rest of its body stood out from the snow captured my imagination instantly. After an obliterating blizzard the fresh snow lay deep, this turning the somewhat muddy landscape that surrounded the local village of Islip into a winter wonderland. I took this photo after putting out bird feed, which attracted many garden birds – one of which being this magnificent robin.

📷 **Sony A350, Sigma 70–300mm f/4-5.6 APO DG MACRO**

▲ **JAMIE UNWIN – AGED 15**   FINALIST *PLANT PORTRAITS*
Withered Daisies
Oxford Botanical Gardens, England.

My mum and I went to the Oxford Botanical Gardens on a grey autumn day. I was looking for interesting subjects to photograph that would capture the change in seasons. I felt these fading daisies conveyed this message well.

📷 **Sony A350, Sigma 70–300mm f/4-5.6 APO DG MACRO**

International Garden Photographer of the Year supported
the MuckIn4Life campaign run by Defra.

▲ JAMIE GREEN   NORTHERN SECTION WINNER

Burning Brush

The photo was taken by Voluntary Ranger, Jamie Green, at Rusland Mosses, Rusland valley, in the Lake District National Park.

The photo shows a raised estuarine mire, of national importance, that has been taken over by invasive scrub and trees which were drying out the mosses.

Volunteers in the photo were collecting the scrub and previously felled branches for burning on site. This helps return the mosses to their original habitat and allows the water levels increase.

The Lake District National park encourages volunteers from all walks of life to get involved in their conservation work.

▲ MIKE TURNER   NORTHERN SECTION – RUNNER-UP

Very Technical

This photo was taken by volunteer Mike Turner and shows two other volunteers, Phil Dover and Malcolm Wade, along with Val Edmondson, a National Park Ranger repairing dry stone walls at Bowness Knott near Ennerdale Water in the Lake District National Park.

Dry stone walls, practical yet attractive field boundaries, are built without mortar or cement. This allows the wall to settle into the landscape, and gives strength and resilience to survive harsh climates and frosts. There are many benefits to dry stone walls including sheltering crops, livestock and buildings and preventing soil erosion. They also provide nesting and perching sites for birds and roosting holes for bats, they are germinating sites for plants, are superb surfaces for mosses and lichens and they harbour insects and reptiles in their holes, nooks and crannies.

The campaign aims to increase the number and diversity of people involved in conservation volunteering, while also increasing awareness and understanding that being active outdoors, whether in urban green spaces or the natural environment, has physical and mental health benefits.

 ILENE STERNS   SOUTHERN SECTION WINNER. OVERALL WINNER

Rhododendron clearing on Lundy Island

Ilene Sterns entered a photo of a group of Lundy Field Society volunteers 'rhodi bashing' on the East side of Lundy Island. Lundy Island is in the Bristol Channel, between England and Wales. Ilene Sterns is a regular visitor to the island and a contributor to other conservation projects including bird and seal recording.

'Rhodi bashing' involves cutting down the invasive rhododendron. It encourages the re-growth of the rare Lundy Cabbage, a plant which grows only on the East side of Lundy Island. The Lundy Cabbage supports two endemic species, the Lundy Cabbage Beetle and the Lundy Cabbage Weevil, which live only on this plant so cannot survive without it.

The 'rhodi bashing' project has been going on for several years; it depends largely on volunteers and is a challenging task as it involves hard work on steep slopes, often in harsh weather. The project has already demonstrated real results, Lundy Cabbage is beginning to grow back in areas where it has not been seen for many years.

BERYL HEATON   SOUTHERN SECTION RUNNER UP

Bulb Planting

Beryl Heaton is the treasurer of Malago Valley Conservation Group known locally as MVCG in South West Bristol which has been in existence for 15 years.

The group campaigns to improve the area by acting as a pressure group, undertaking practical action to make things better and arranging talks, walks and other events.

This picture shows Daffodil bulb planting near Highridge Common with several MVCG volunteers.